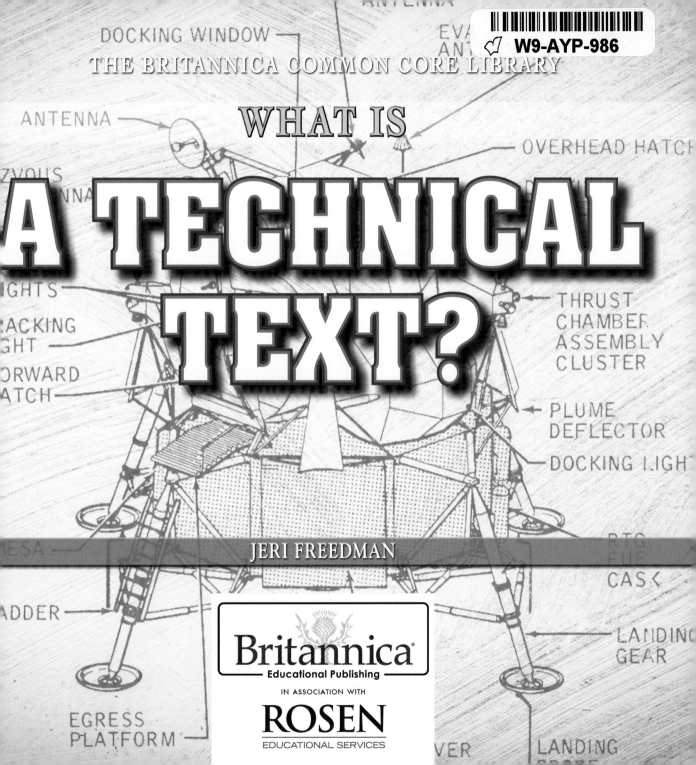

THE BRITANNICA COMMON CORE LIBRARY

WHAT IS A TECHNICAL TEXT?

JERI FREEDMAN

Britannica®
Educational Publishing

IN ASSOCIATION WITH

ROSEN
EDUCATIONAL SERVICES

Published in 2015 by Britannica Educational Publishing (a trademark of Encyclopædia Britannica, Inc.) in association with The Rosen Publishing Group, Inc.
29 East 21st Street, New York, NY 10010

Distributed exclusively by Rosen Publishing.
To see additional Britannica Educational Publishing titles, go to rosenpublishing.com.

First Edition

Britannica Educational Publishing
J. E. Luebering: Director, Core Reference Group
Mary Rose McCudden: Editor, Britannica Student Encyclopedia

Rosen Publishing
Hope Lourie Killcoyne: Executive Editor
Nelson Sá: Art Director
Michael Moy: Designer
Cindy Reiman: Photography Manager
Karen Huang: Photo Researcher

Library of Congress Cataloging-in-Publication Data

Freedman, Jeri.
What is a technical text?/Jeri Freedman. — First edition.
    pages cm. — (The Britannica common core library)
Includes bibliographical references and index.
ISBN 978-1-62275-672-8 (library bound) — ISBN 978-1-62275-673-5 (pbk.) — ISBN 978-1-62275-674-2 (6-pack)
1. Technical literature—Juvenile literature. 2. Technical writing—Juvenile literature. I. Title.
T10.7F74 2015
600—dc23

2014020385

Manufactured in the United States of America

Photo credits:

Cover (background) © iStockphoto.com/marcoventuriniautieri; cover (hands and tablet) © iStockphoto.com/Anatoliy Babiy; cover (tablet screen) © iStockphoto.com/elgol; p.1, interior pages background image Diagram of the Apollo Lunar Module. Courtesy of NASA History Office; p. 4 Mark Hall/The Image Bank/Getty Images; pp. 5, 17 Encyclopædia Britannica, Inc.; pp. 6, 9, 12, 13, 22, 24, 27 © Rosen Publishing; p. 7 © iStockphoto.com/Timothy Masters; p. 8 Mikko Lemola/Shutterstock. com; p. 14 Andresr/Shutterstock.com; p. 15 A and N photography/Shutterstock.com; p. 16 Christopher Futcher/E+/Getty Images; p. 18 Mathew Ward/Dorling Kindersley/Getty Images; p. 19 Diana Haronis/Moment/Getty Images; p. 20 oliveromg/ Shutterstock.com; p. 21 Thierry Foulon/PhotoAlto Agency RF/Getty Images; p. 25 AP Images for Macy's; p. 29 Hurst Photo/ Shutterstock.com.

CONTENTS

What Is a Technical Text?

A technical text is a special type of nonfiction. It is meant to teach readers something new about a topic. It often instructs readers on how to perform a task.

Technical texts can be found everywhere. Instruction booklets or leaflets that come with household items are technical texts. These can include instructions for how to play a game.

Labels on machinery that contain safety warnings and operating instructions are technical texts. Recipes and other useful how-to information are common technical texts found on the Internet or in books.

A technical text often tells how to do something, such as how to set up a tent.

> **Labels** are words or names on something to describe or show what it is.

A technical text may explain how to perform an experiment or make a stuffed animal. It can describe how to fit together the parts of a robot or build a tree house. Technical texts are made for readers who are learning something new. Therefore, they must present information so that it is easy to understand.

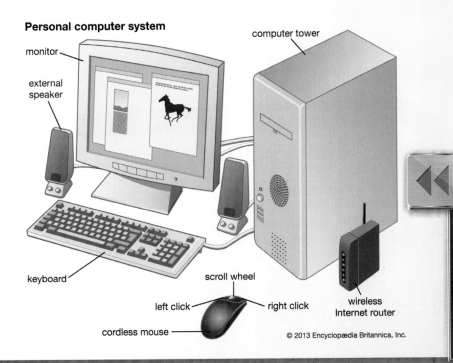

Personal computer system

computer tower

monitor

external speaker

keyboard

scroll wheel

left click

right click

cordless mouse

wireless Internet router

© 2013 Encyclopædia Britannica, Inc.

Labels show the parts of a personal computer system. A technical text can explain how to put together the parts of a personal computer system.

What Qualities Does a Technical Text Have?

To help people learn new skills and ideas, technical writing must have the following qualities.

Clear and Compact Writing

Technical texts use language that is easy to understand. Short, simple words and sentences are used. Only necessary information is included. The words are organized to help readers

A technical text uses bullets, or dots, in a list to make clear the most important points.

Safe Strength Training

As with any activity, strength training can result in injury. You can reduce your risk of injury by taking part in a well-supervised strength-training program with a qualified adult. Listening and following instructions will also help prevent injury, as will the following tips:

- Be sure to wear appropriate clothing and closed-toe athletic shoes.
- Start your workout with a five- to ten-minute warm-up. Walking, running in place, or jumping rope are good options.
- If you are training with machines, make sure they have been adjusted for your height.

Graphs are drawings that show mathematical information with lines, shapes, and colors. **Diagrams** are drawings that explain or show the parts of something.

understand the topic. Information is given in the order that it is needed.

Helpful Presentation

Technical texts often use design elements to highlight important points. These elements can include bullet points, numbered lists, headings, boldface, underline, and blank space. Visual aids, such as tables, charts, maps, **graphs**, and other **diagrams**, are also used to illustrate important ideas from the text.

Diagrams help to guide a person in putting together an object, such as a birdhouse.

Reader Awareness

The goal of every technical text is to teach the reader something specific. To do this, technical writers must understand what their audience needs to know. Information that is new to the reader is defined.

Technical texts are not meant to entertain readers. The writing must have a serious tone, or feeling. The reader will know to pay close attention to the information in the text.

Correct Information

People use technical texts to do important jobs. Some of these jobs, like fixing a car, can produce dangerous conditions when they are not done correctly. Errors in technical

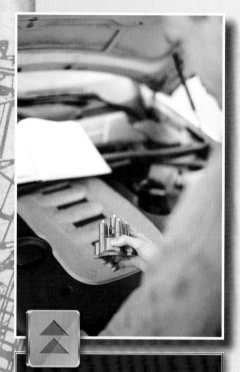

Car repair manuals are instruction booklets that mechanics often use when they fix cars.

Technical Writers

The World Record Paper Airplane Book (2006), by engineers Ken Blackburn and Jeff Lammers, teaches readers how to fold and fly different types of paper airplanes—as well as why airplanes fly and crash.

writing can cause physical injury, damage to property, or misunderstandings.

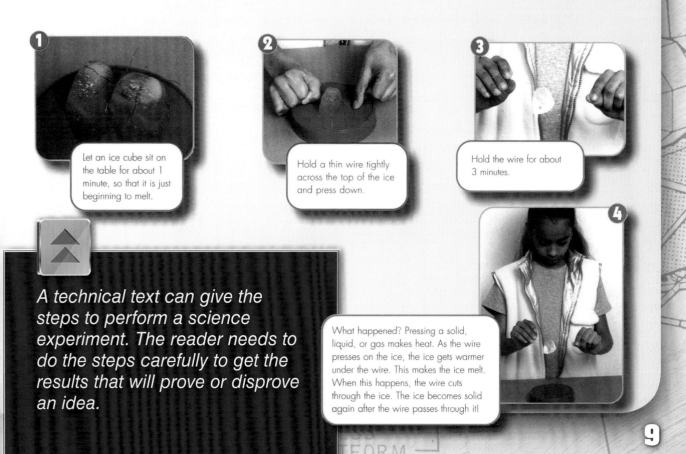

1 Let an ice cube sit on the table for about 1 minute, so that it is just beginning to melt.

2 Hold a thin wire tightly across the top of the ice and press down.

3 Hold the wire for about 3 minutes.

4 What happened? Pressing a solid, liquid, or gas makes heat. As the wire presses on the ice, the ice gets warmer under the wire. This makes the ice melt. When this happens, the wire cuts through the ice. The ice becomes solid again after the wire passes through it!

A technical text can give the steps to perform a science experiment. The reader needs to do the steps carefully to get the results that will prove or disprove an idea.

Technical Text in Use

The following examples show how technical texts present information differently for different purposes.

A Scientific Study

A scientific study examines events to explain their effects on the world. It often includes mathematical information. Graphs, or charts, are used to compare amounts of things. The most common kinds of graphs are circle graphs (or pie charts), **bar graphs**, and line graphs. The passage below uses a bar graph and a

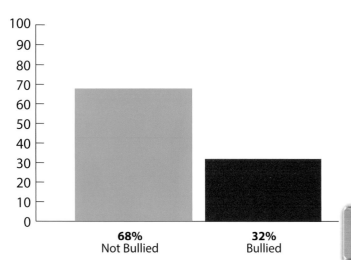

Percentage of Students Bullied and Not Bullied

68%
Not Bullied

32%
Bullied

A bar chart shows the percent of students who were bullied and not bullied while at school.

pie chart to show how bullying affects groups of students.

According to the National Center for Education Statistics, in 2007, 32 percent of students from 12 to 18 years old reported having been bullied at school during the school year. Of those, 11 percent said that they were pushed, shoved, tripped, or spit on. Four percent said that someone tried to make them do things they did not want to do or that their property was destroyed on purpose.

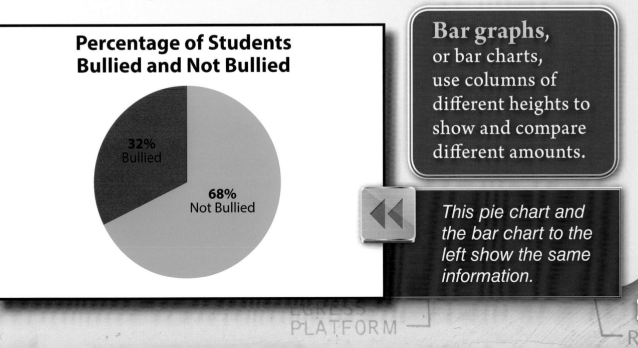

Percentage of Students Bullied and Not Bullied

32% Bullied

68% Not Bullied

Bar graphs, or bar charts, use columns of different heights to show and compare different amounts.

This pie chart and the bar chart to the left show the same information.

A Scientific Experiment

A scientific experiment involves a series of actions and observations to test an idea. Below is an experiment dealing with the evaporation of water from a carrot. Evaporation is a process through which a liquid changes to a gas. Vegetables, fruit, and other plant products often contain liquid water.

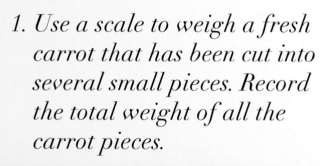

1. *Use a scale to weigh a fresh carrot that has been cut into several small pieces. Record the total weight of all the carrot pieces.*

Following specific steps and making careful observations while doing a scientific experiment allow you to test an idea.

2. Set the carrot pieces out on a paper plate for several days.

3. Weigh the carrot pieces a second time and record their total weight.

4. Compare the new weight of the carrot to the weight you recorded earlier.

Steps in an experiment are usually numbered to help readers do them in the correct order.

Technical Writers

Writer Sy Montgomery and illustrator Nic Bishop show readers a scientific study in the book *Kakapo Rescue: Saving the World's Strangest Parrot* (2010).

Let's Compare

Studies and experiments are two methods used by scientists. Both provide the reader with **data**, or pieces of information.

The bullying study reports findings to the reader. It does not expect the reader to do part of the study or any task related to the study. All of the information that the reader is expected to consider is included in the text. The study also includes visual aids to help the reader understand

People often gather information when making a scientific study. That information can be examined and used to explain ideas about the world.

> **Data** are facts or measurements used to explain ideas.

By following the steps for doing an experiment, scientists can prove whether or not their ideas about what should happen are true.

the mathematical information.

The second example provides the steps for the reader to conduct an experiment. The steps involved in the experiment are numbered so that the reader can do them in the correct order. Readers are expected to gather and interpret the information from the experiment themselves.

How to Play Volleyball

The following passage describes the main rules of volleyball.

Play begins when one player serves. A player serves by hitting the ball over to the receiving team's side of the net. The receiving team tries to return the serve, or hit the ball back over the net. Players may hit the ball with any part of the body above the waist as long as the ball is clearly hit and not held. Each team may hit the ball up to three times before sending it back over the net. The serving team

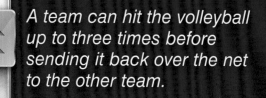

A team can hit the volleyball up to three times before sending it back over the net to the other team.

Technical Writers

Writers Abigael McIntyre, Sandra Giddens, and Owen Giddens explain to readers how to play and train for the game of volleyball in *An Insider's Guide to Volleyball* (2015).

scores a point if the other team fails to return the ball or hits it out of bounds. When the serving team fails to return the ball or hits it out of bounds, it loses the serve to the other team. A winning score is at least fifteen points, with at least a two-point lead.

VOLLEYBALL COURT

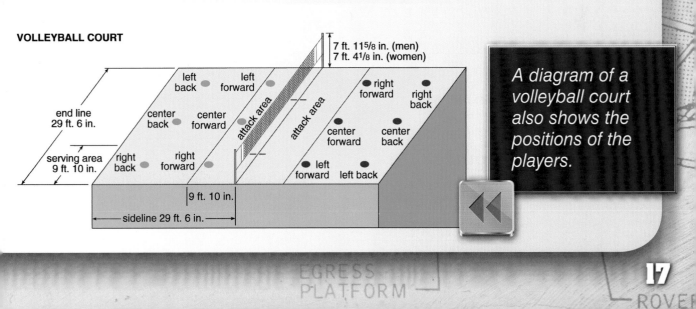

A diagram of a volleyball court also shows the positions of the players.

How to Play Checkers

Games often include **manuals** or instruction leaflets that explain all of their rules. The following passage describes some of the rules of playing checkers.

The game is played by two people. The players move disc-shaped pieces around a game board that has alternating squares of black and some other color.

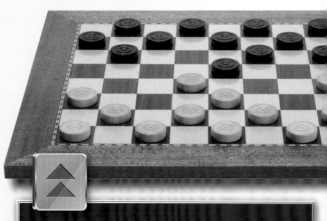

Step 1: The players place twelve game pieces each on the black squares in three rows at opposite sides of the board.

Step 2: One player starts by moving one of the pieces

A checkerboard is marked with squares of two different colors. Each player uses different colored game pieces called checkers.

> **Manuals** are small books that give useful information about how to use something.

in the row farthest from the edge of the board. The player can move the piece only one square at a time. The player can only move forward, and the move must be diagonal so that the piece ends up on another black square.

The game of checkers is played by two people. Players can move only one game piece at a time.

Let's Compare

The passages about volleyball and checkers give important information about how to play each game and use illustrations to highlight the text. However, each set of directions is organized differently.

The passage about how to play volleyball gives only the basic rules of the game. It is written for an audience that is unfamiliar with the sport. After reading the passage, the reader will be able to start playing. Although all of the information is important for the reader to know, the reader is not required to follow the instructions in a particular order.

The text example for how to play volleyball gives the basic rules for playing the game. Players do not have to follow the directions in a particular order after serving the ball.

The passage about how to play checkers presents information in an order that must be followed. The first two sentences appear first because they describe what is needed for any game to take place: two players, a checkerboard, and game pieces. Step 1 must be done before Step 2.

In the game of checkers, players have to complete Step 1 before going on to Step 2 when playing the game.

A Recipe for Hot Chocolate

This recipe for Mexican hot chocolate includes a **safety warning** to young people about using a stove and getting a grown-up to help.

Ingredients
½ cup (120 ml) sugar
¼ cup (60 ml) cocoa
¼ teaspoon salt
1 tablespoon all-purpose flour
1 teaspoon cinnamon
1 cup (240 ml) cold water
4 cups (1 l) milk
2 teaspoons vanilla extract

1. *Place the sugar, cocoa, salt, flour, cinnamon, and water in a large pot. Place the pot over low heat, and stir until the mixture dissolves into the water.*

◀◀

Recipes are technical texts that help people create their own tasty treats.

Instructions often contain a **safety warning**. These warnings are often placed in a box, colored circle, or other shape so that they are easily noticed. It is important to follow safety warnings so that no one gets hurt.

2. *After the mixture is dissolved, turn the stove up to medium high. Stir the mixture until it boils. Boil for three to five minutes, stirring all the time.*
3. *Add the milk. Continue to stir until the milk is hot but not boiling.*
4. *Just before the milk boils, remove the pot from the heat. Stir in the vanilla extract, and serve!*

When cooking, you should always have an adult with you in the kitchen to help. Many of the tools used to prepare these recipes and others can be dangerous. Always be very careful when using a knife or a stove.

Take special care to notice and read any safety warnings that appear in technical texts. Ask an adult that you know to read the warning label and help you complete the task.

How to Make a Mask

This example shows the first few steps in how to make a simple cat mask.

1. *Draw a circle around a plate to make a circle of cardboard about 8 inches (20 cm) across. Cut out the circle.*
2. *Cut out eyeholes the same distance apart as your own eyes. Cut a flap for your nose.*
3. *With a glue stick, stick blue paper to the cardboard to cover it. Stick pink eyes cut from paper around the eyeholes. Cut out cardboard ears and stick them on.*

This photograph helps readers see how each numbered step adds to the finished cat mask. It also shows readers what the finished mask should look like.

Technical Writers

Martha Stewart is famous for her homemaking arts and crafts. Her business produced a number of arts and crafts books, including *Martha Stewart's Favorite Crafts for Kids: 175 Projects for Kids of All Ages to Create, Build, Design, Explore, and Share.*

4. Cut out a mouth, tongue, and some little circles from paper and stick them on. Glue on pieces of drinking straw for whiskers.

Martha Stewart explains how to make holiday popcorn balls. Stewart enjoys cooking and crafts and has written many books and articles on those subjects.

Let's Compare

Recipes and craft directions usually follow a similar style of **presentation**. Materials or ingredients are listed first. Then the directions for how to make the dish or craft follow in numbered steps. Presenting the directions in this way is important because steps need to be done in the correct order.

Recipes and craft directions often use visual aids differently. Craft directions usually include illustrations or photographs that show how to do each step described in the text. Recipes normally do not illustrate each numbered step. They sometimes show a photograph of the raw ingredients, especially if they are unusual or hard to find in stores. Most often recipes will have a photograph of the finished dish only. Both recipes and craft instructions may contain warnings about any possible dangers involved with the task.

The **presentation** of recipes or directions means the way in which the information is shown, described, or explained.

Ingredients

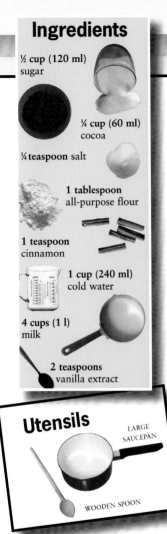

½ cup (120 ml) sugar

¼ cup (60 ml) cocoa

¼ teaspoon salt

1 tablespoon all-purpose flour

1 teaspoon cinnamon

1 cup (240 ml) cold water

4 cups (1 l) milk

2 teaspoons vanilla extract

Utensils

LARGE SAUCEPAN

WOODEN SPOON

1 Place the sugar, cocoa, salt, flour, cinnamon, and water in a large saucepan. Place the saucepan over low heat and stir until the mixture **dissolves** into the water.

2 After the mixture is dissolved, turn the stove up to medium high. Stir the mixture until it boils. Boil for 3 to 5 minutes, stirring all the time.

3 Add the milk. Continue to stir until the milk is hot but not boiling.

4 Just before the milk boils, remove the saucepan from the heat. Stir in the vanilla extract, and serve!

Some recipes include visual aids for every ingredient, tool, and step that is needed. Here are visual aids for the Mexican hot chocolate recipe.

Write Your Own Technical Text

Now it is your turn to write a technical text. Your text should tell someone how to make an object, complete an experiment, or do a task. Follow these steps:

1. Pick your topic. Choose something that you already know how to do well and that someone else might enjoy learning how to do.
2. Choose your audience. Will your audience know much about the topic? What will they need you to define?
3. Write an introduction to the activity that includes important points and definitions.
4. Write the steps to do the activity.
5. Draw or print pictures to help the reader understand the directions.

6. Put what you wrote aside for a day. Next reread it as if you were the audience. Is any information missing, unnecessary, or incorrect?

7. Have some fun! Ask someone you know to follow your directions. Can he or she do it?

By watching classmates follow your directions, you will learn whether your technical text is clear and correct.

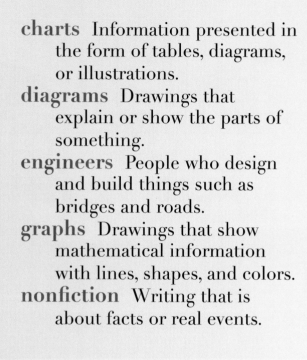

charts Information presented in the form of tables, diagrams, or illustrations.

diagrams Drawings that explain or show the parts of something.

engineers People who design and build things such as bridges and roads.

graphs Drawings that show mathematical information with lines, shapes, and colors.

nonfiction Writing that is about facts or real events.

observations Acts of careful watching and listening to gather information.

tables Information displayed in forms that often include rows and columns.

technical Relating to the practical use of machines or science in industry, medicine, and other fields.

visual aids Illustrations or diagrams that make a text easier to understand.

Books

Blackburn, Ken, and Jeff Lammers. *The World Record Paper Airplane Book.* New York, NY: Workman Publishing, 2007.

Martha Stewart Living editors. *Martha Stewart's Favorite Crafts for Kids: 175 Projects for Kids of All Ages to Create, Build, Design, Explore, and Share.* New York, NY: Potter Craft, 2013.

McIntyre, Abigael, Sandra Giddens, and Owen Giddens. *An Insider's Guide to Volleyball.* New York, NY: Rosen Publishing Group, 2015.

Montgomery, Sy. *Kakapo Rescue: Saving the World's Strangest Parrot.* New York, NY: Houghton Mifflin Books for Children, 2010.

Oxlade, Chris. *The Science and History Project Book.* Helotes, TX: Armadillo Books, 2013.

Ward, Karen. *Fun with Mexican Cooking.* New York, NY: Rosen Publishing Group, 2010.

Williams, Zella. *Experiments with Solids, Liquids, and Gases.* New York, NY: Rosen Publishing Group, 2007.

Websites

Because of the changing nature of Internet links, Rosen Publishing has developed an online list of websites related to the subject of this book. This site is updated regularly. Please use this link to access the list:

http://www.rosenlinks.com/BCCL/Tech

INDEX